Internet Marketing for Your Small Business

Everything You Need to Know to Get Started NOW

By Carol R. Harkins

Copyright © 2012 Carol R. Harkins

All rights reserved.

ISBN: 1467949388
ISBN-13: 978-1467949385

DEDICATION

To my mother, with deep love and appreciation.
You are amazing!

CONTENTS

Introduction i

1	Why Internet Marketing?.............	1
2	Your Business Website...................	7
3	How to Choose Keywords..............	15
4	Search Engine Optimization...........	27
5	Google Webmaster Account.........	35
6	Google Analytics.............................	51
7	Google Places and Local Search....	69
8	Online Reviews...............................	83
9	Article Marketing............................	91
10	Video Marketing..............................	99
11	Blogs and Why You Need One.......	107
12	Mobile Marketing............................	117
13	Paid Advertising (PPC)....................	131
14	Summary	141

INTRODUCTION

Most small business owners know they need the Internet to market their businesses. Some already own websites and have garnered top positions in Google for their keyword niches. Others have been burned by unethical web marketers, or are fearful of the technology because they don't understand it. For all business owners, Internet marketing keeps changing so rapidly that it's difficult to keep pace and still run their business.

This book is for small business owners who aren't sure where to start, who want to do it themselves, or who want to educate themselves to effectively communicate with a hired web professional.

We can't guarantee your results, even if you follow the recommendations in this book. We can guarantee that you will have the tools to make better decisions about your Internet marketing. Our goal is to help you use your web presence to get more clients and customers, and ultimately make more money for your successful business.

1 Why Internet Marketing?

The Internet has been around since 1969, but it's only been in the past 20 years that businesses have used it commercially. Although the World Wide Web was invented by Tim Berners-Lee in 1990, it was a text-based application. In 1993, when the Mosaic browser was released with the ability to transmit images, businesses began to see the Web's commercial possibilities.

Today, our society has embraced the Web as though it was always a part of us. We go online to check movie times and sports scores, to make purchases, and to look up contact information for local businesses. Some of us do all of the above, and more, from our smartphones. But did you know that 83% of people first search online before making a local product or service purchase? And 98% of searchers choose a business on Page 1 of the search?

If your business is not coming up on Page 1, you are losing out to your competition which is already there!

What's wrong with traditional marketing?

Many businesses are holding on to the "tried and true" marketing venues of the past, like the Yellow Pages. Unfortunately, most people aren't using the Yellow Pages anymore – except maybe as doorstops or booster seats for small visiting children. Yellow Pages are no longer the best use of your marketing dollars: you create and publish your ad, which then remains static until next year when you're able to make changes. Contrast that with your online presence which can be updated and changed as quickly and frequently as you want.

Who receives the Yellow Pages? Answer: Residences and businesses with landline telephones. According to the Pew Research Center in 2010, a quarter of today's households do not have landlines. That means 25% of your potential market doesn't even have the option of looking at your Yellow Pages ad at home!

The owners of the print Yellow Pages directories know all this, and while they have tried to take their information online, they can't compete favorably with Google. No matter how much you pay for a Yellow Pages ad placement, you will not have the traffic seeing that ad, or clicking through to your offer or website to do business with you. That's because Google currently has about 65% of the U.S. search market, Yahoo! and Bing each have about 15%, and the Yellow Pages, along with all the other search websites, make up the final 4.5%. Do you want to spend your money on the Yellow Pages now?

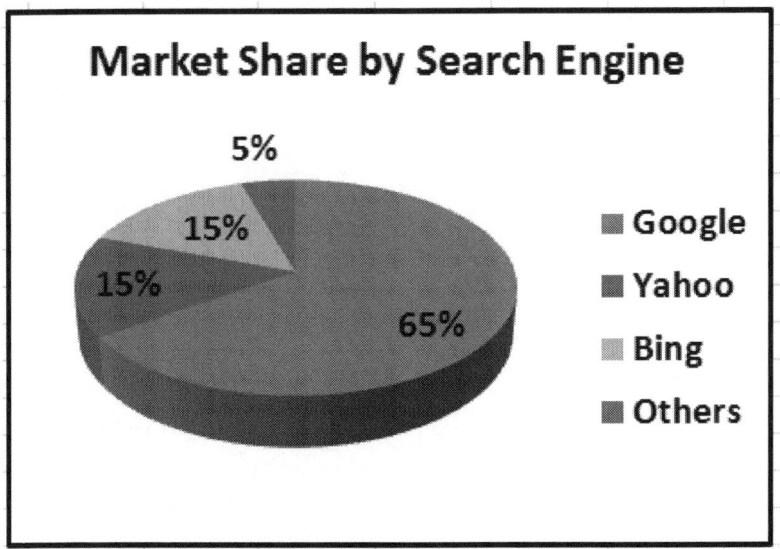

Source: ComScore Dec. 2011

We're not saying that the print medium is going away any time soon. There are still many people who like to hold a brochure or business card in their hands. But be careful not to underestimate the change that is sweeping through the business landscape with mobile marketing, social media, and the Internet itself. Historically, businesses that were able to successfully incorporate the new media (newspapers, billboards, radio, television, etc.) into their marketing plans were the ones that continued to thrive.

What should I do next?

So what should you do to get your business online, to take advantage of the Internet in your marketing plan? This book will help guide you through the process of what to do, what works, what doesn't, and why. We are expecting you to participate in this process by completing the workbook exercises at the end of each Chapter. When you're finished, you will have the tools you need to make your website, and the Internet, work for you.

CHAPTER 1: WORKSHEET

What are you currently spending on Marketing?

Advertising	Annual Amount Spent
Newspaper	
Magazine	
Yellow Pages	
Billboard	
Radio	
Television	
Give away items	
Vehicle Wrap	
Apparel	
Other	
Local Print Directories	
Chamber of Commerce	
Professional Organization	
Other	
Business Expo or Event Booth	
Chamber of Commerce	
Other	
Community	
School/Sport Sponsorship	
Coupon Books	
Other	
	.
Other	
Total:	
Average Monthly Budget:	

2 Your Business Website

We are assuming you already have a business website. If you don't, please read this chapter to be sure that the website you create takes into account the steps outlined here.

Your website should be better than your best employee: able to answer questions 24 x 7 x 365, present your business to your prospects and customers from the perspective of what you can do for them, even sell your products any hour of the day or night - at a cost that's a fraction of what you pay that employee.

It's actually fun to do the math. If your best employee earns just $20.00/hour (higher than minimum wage, but lower than the average hourly wages and benefits paid to workers in private industry as reported in December 2011 by the Bureau of Labor Statistics), and worked 24 x 7 x 365, you would end up paying her $1,226,400.00 each year to do what your website does! Your website is actually quite a bargain!

Keep in mind that the main purpose of your website is to increase your bottom line. It may give your business credibility, it may generate leads, it may sell your products. The best website should accomplish all of these.

Today, there are more than 50 billion pages in Google's index (http://www.worldwidewebsize.com/) There are more than one billion Google searches daily. Your website needs to be visible among this vast ocean of information.

Website focus

What do you need to think about when you or someone you hire creates your business website? Back in the mid 1990's, if you even had a business website you were considered "cutting edge." You could have moving text, a wild background, navigation that took your visitors to a dead end where they would have to "back" out because there was no place else to go. If you had a business website back then, it was probably "all about you" and what a great business you had.

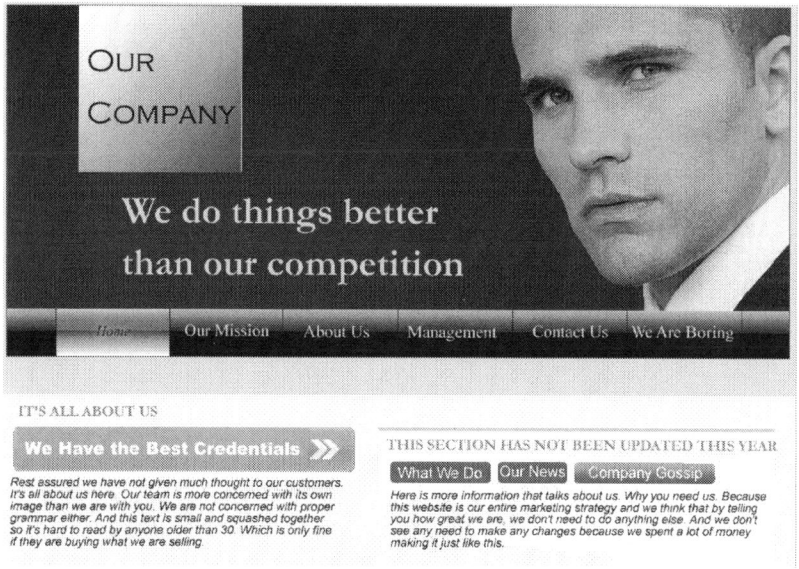

Build the foundation

Things have changed since then. The focus of your website must be on your customers or prospective customers. What can **you** do for **them**? How can **you** serve **them**? What do **they** want? It's so easy to click away from your site, so be sure that you answer these questions before going further. You need to create a persona – a fictional person (or people) who have the qualities of those people you are looking for as customers.

When creating your personas, you'll need to use your imagination. Give them names! Think about where they are from, what are their interests, what makes them buy. You will need to think about these personas as if they were real people, because your marketing efforts are going to target them. The better you know them, the better you will be able to create your marketing pieces – including your website – to attract the customers you want.

Your personas will help you remember that **you** are not the target user or buyer. Everything you create in your marketing process must be done through **their** mindset, not yours.

CHAPTER 2: WORKSHEET

Personas

Before you create your 21st Century website, create at least 2 personas for your prospective customers.

	Persona Name:		
Where do they live?			
Male/Female?			
Education			
Income Level			
Age			
Single/Married/Kids?			
Attitude toward spending?			
Are they religious?			
Do they travel? Where?			
Do they like sports? Which?			
Where do they shop?			
Who influences their buying?			
Where do they look for information (search engine/social media/other)?			
What devices do they use (desktop/laptop/library/mobile)?			

What frustrates them?		
What do they need?		
What do they want?		

CAROL R HARKINS

3 How to Choose Keywords

What are keywords anyway, and why are they so important?

Can't I just use whatever words that describe my products or services?

Keywords are the phrases that people type into a search engine, in order to receive a ranked list of web pages dealing with that topic. Every page on your website should have at most two keywords that you are targeting, so that people searching for that topic will be presented with your page.

Many small business owners have heard about a "keyword tag" on the back side of their website where they believe all the words that describe their products or services need to be written. That was the way it was done in the '90s.

Today, we suggest that you ignore the META keyword tag.

Don't make the mistake of thinking that YOU know what keywords are going to bring you traffic. Yes, YOU know your business. YOU are the best person to create your initial list of candidate keywords. BUT often the phrases that you think might be your best keywords turn out to be just the opposite. (see roofers example below)

Keywords are the building blocks of search. Get them wrong and you've just wasted a lot of time and possibly money. Get them right and you'll see the results in your business' bottom line.

Keyword research

The truth is, you need to do some research to be sure that the keywords you want to target are:

- actually being searched for by enough people
- not unrealistically competitive
- being used by people who are ready to act, not just by researchers or "tire kickers"

You should start with a seed list of words that your persona (see Chapter 2) might type in if s/he were looking for your products or services. Brainstorm with your employees and ask some of your current customers. You might be surprised by what they tell you!

Next, use the Google Keywords Tool. Google has been known to change the address for this, so we recommend that you just Google "Google Keywords Tool." The Google tool is the same one that is used for AdWords (paid search) and we'll explain how to take this into account when searching for non-paid keywords.

Our objective here is to find phrases (1 in diagram next page) that have a good number of Local Monthly Searches (2), without being overly competitive (3). The competition measure used here is for Pay Per Click, but that also gives us a gauge as to how competitive the keyword is in general.

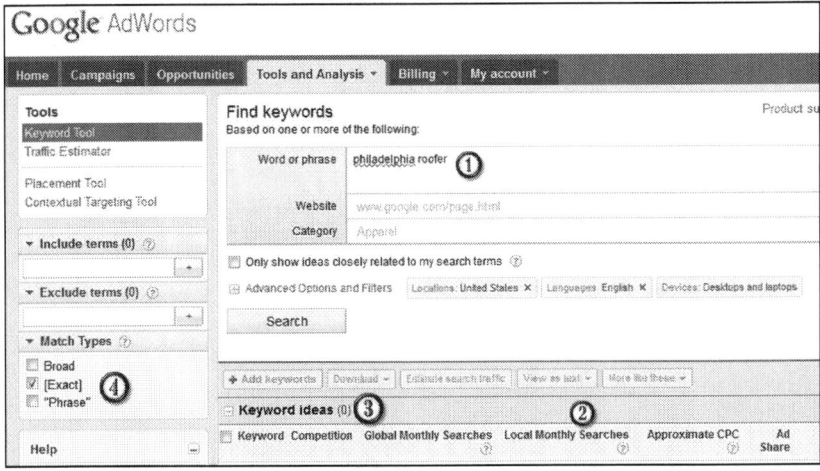

Be sure to select "Exact Match" (4) as the Match Type in the left column. This will limit our results to people who are searching on the exact keyword phrase we are researching. Broad Match will return significantly more results because it includes your words in any order, possibly with words between them, plus related words. The keyword "brass decorative pitcher" would match "decorative pitcher" as well as "brass pitcher photos." Broad Match is great for Adwords, but not for our purpose.

Likewise, Phrase Match needs all the words in the correct order, but can have other words included as well.

Exact Match gives you just what you ask for – so this is the most accurate representation of how well a keyword might actually perform for you. Remember, your site might come up as a search result, but if it's not what the searcher was looking for, they won't click through to your site, and most likely they won't buy from you.

Below is a search for **Philadelphia roofer**. Since we are using a local term, the Global and Local Monthly values are mostly the same. That keyword is showing 46 monthly searches. But if you were a Philadelphia roofer, wouldn't you rather target **Philadelphia roofers** or **roofing Philadelphia**, since each would bring you almost four times the traffic? But you wouldn't know that without the research.

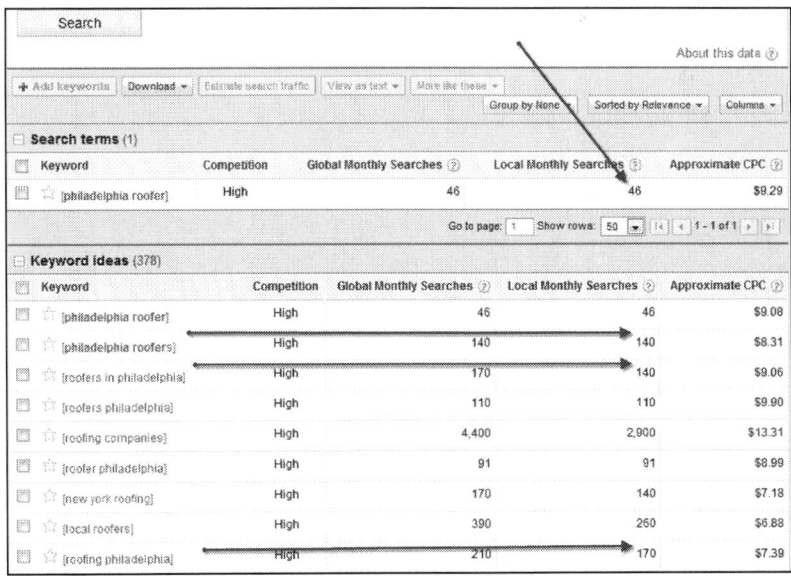

You also need to understand that the Monthly Search number is an estimate of how many searches will be done for that phrase. But even if you rank Number 1 for the keyword, the best you will actually get is somewhere between 40 – 50% of that number. This is because that number includes Pay Per Click, Image, Video and other types of searches.

Evaluating the competition

At this stage, you may want to stay away from targeting keywords which are designated as High competition. Following this example, the keyword **quality roofing** is showing 590 Local Monthly searches while being of Medium competition. It would be worth having a page on your website targeting that phrase.

Another way to judge the competition is to look at Google's search results for that phrase. These websites are your actual competition. In order to get on Page 1, you have to push one of these sites off. Check them out. Are they already well-optimized? Are they educational (.edu) or government (.gov) sites? If you answered yes to either of those questions, then those sites are going to be difficult to overcome, at least at this point in your website's career.

Quantity of competition

How many pages are already indexed by Google for your prospective keyword? That's another factor you'll want to consider. Search on the phrase in quotes to get the best approximation of this value. Even if those pages are not well-optimized, Google gives existing pages more credit than it does to new pages. Ideally, we'd like to find keywords for which there are a million monthly searches, but only 10 pages in the index for that phrase. Unfortunately that's not going to happen! But the fewer competing pages relative to the number of actual searches, the better.

Finding additional keywords

You've probably already discovered that single words make for poor candidates. What happens when you've exhausted your seed list and still aren't satisfied with what's left? Google itself can help you find additional keywords that you'll want to utilize on your site. Type your main keyword into Google, hit search, and then in the left column click on Show search tools, then click on Related Searches. This will display a list of other phrases you should consider targeting on separate pages of your website.

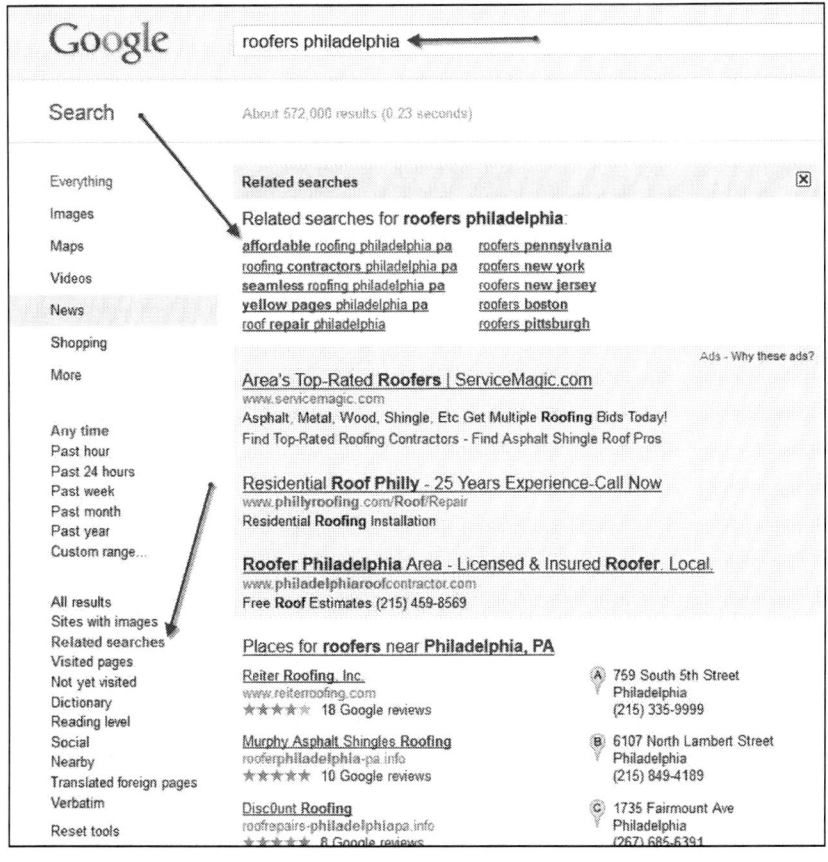

CHAPTER 3: WORKSHEET

Keywords

Website Name : _____

Website URL : _____

Main idea of site (e.g., plumbing services, cosmetic dentistry, landscaping, etc.)

_____

Fill in the chart below with your seed keywords. Add keywords to the list as you research and find new ones. Use **Related Searches** to identify additional candidates. Put a **Star** in the right column for the keywords you are going to target.

Keyword	# Local Monthly Searches	Competition (High/ Medium/ Low)	# Pages indexed in Google	Star

CAROL R HARKINS

4 Search Engine Optimization

How a search engine works

How does a search engine perform its magic? First, it sends out "bots" or "spiders" to collect information about your website. These spiders are automated computer programs that normally start on your homepage, collecting information regarding just what your website is about. They can only read the text on your site (both the text that humans can read, as well as the text on the back side of the page) but they cannot tell whether that gorgeous image on the page is a duck or a doorway. That's why **all important information needs to be textual**.

The spider will also collect information about what links are on the homepage, and will then try to visit each linked page to decide what that page is all about.

Once the spider has completed its data collection and returns it to the search engine, the search engine performs an analysis of the information. Using a very complex and secret combination of rules, the search engine decides how important each page is relative to other pages which have the same topic.

Finally, when a visitor comes to the search engine to perform his search, he is given the results in the order which was determined by the search engine's rules.

How to optimize a page

Now that you have your keywords, you need to be sure that your website contains those keywords in the proper way. **A webpage will not be listed on the results page unless it contains the keywords that are being searched for**.

Each page can be optimized for at most, one or two phrases. The keyword phrase needs to best describe what that particular page is about. Make a list of your pages and match up the keywords with the pages you will associate with them.

The most important places to have your keywords are in the Title and Description tags. Be sure that every Title and Description is different for each page on your website.

Next, include the keywords in the headings and subheadings on the page. You also need them in the body of the page. Be careful not to overdo it, or Google will penalize you for "keyword stuffing" – a big no-no.

Finally, be sure that you use the keywords on other pages, both within your website and on other websites, as anchor text to link to the page.

On page optimization

Search Engine Optimization is a vital part of your marketing plan. This piece is often called "on page" optimization and it is something that **you as the site owner have total control** over. Do understand that Google is continually changing and "tweaking" their rules, or algorithm, used to decide whose website should be displayed first. Google doesn't publish their rules, but it is possible to determine what is important, and what isn't, by reading the information that they do publish. Following Matt Cutts (currently the head of Google's Webspam team whose blog is famous in SEO circles) is also valuable. You will need to stay tuned to this area and be ready to change your pages, if warranted, when Google changes their algorithm.

Off page optimization

A few short years ago, proper on page optimization was enough to keep a site on Page One of the search results. Today, you may be competing with thousands of websites that are 100% optimized for the same keyword phrase that you are targeting. What to do? Now we must also focus on off page optimization. Google looks at links to your site from other reputable websites as "votes" for your site.

Since there is no limit to the number of votes your site might get, you will need to concentrate on this area. Chapters 7 through 10 discuss methods that you should use to get links back to your site, including

Google Places and Local Search, Online Reviews, Article Marketing, and Video Marketing. There are many other methods which you can employ, including Citations, Press Releases, Social Bookmarking, Forum Posting, Blog Commenting, and Link Wheels, which are beyond the scope of this book.

Use the structure you create for this Chapter's worksheet to build your optimized website.

CHAPTER 4: WORKSHEET

Optimization

First write your page names down the left column. Then match up your keywords with the pages. You don't have to have keywords for every page. For example, Contact Us won't have enough content meat in order to rank well. But you should still create a unique Title and Description for it. If you have keywords left over, these are great candidates for additional pages – or for additional content that you will add over time.

Page name	Keyword	Title (70 characters max)	Description (160 characters max)

INTERNET MARKETING FOR YOUR SMALL BUSINESS

CAROL R HARKINS

5 Google Webmaster Account

So now you have a website and you've optimized it for Google. The next step is to determine how well that site is performing. Actually this is not a "check it off and on to the next step" because you will want to continue monitoring your website's performance on a regular basis!

Google provides a variety of tools that can help you see how your site is doing and what you might want to change. Google's Webmaster Tools are free and allow you to see some of what Google sees when they go to your site. You can:

- see information on your site's configuration
- see how others are interacting with your site on the web

- specify your "primary" site (with or without the "www")
- tell Google that you have an XML sitemap (Important! More on this below.)
- get diagnostics and suggestions for better site optimization
- and more.

There is also a section called "Labs" where Google tests new tools. These tools may find their way into the mainstream toolset, or you may find they are gone the next time you log in to your account!

There is a lot available in this section, and we are going to start off with the basics. Google provides links to helpful information on each page, so once you complete this chapter, you'll want to go back to your Webmaster Account on a regular basis and learn more about the tools and your site.

Let's get started!

Access your Google Webmaster Account at http://www.google.com/webmasters/tools. If you already have a Google account (like yourname@gmail.com), use it to log in. Otherwise, click on the link at the top of the page to "Sign up for a new Google Account." Then return to this page and log in.

Add and verify your website

The first thing you will need to do when you get there is to add your site. Google offers many links to answer questions they think you might have on each screen, but at this point it's a simple process. Just click on the red "ADD A SITE" button (1). Then type in the URL of your website, for example, www.yoursite.com. (2)

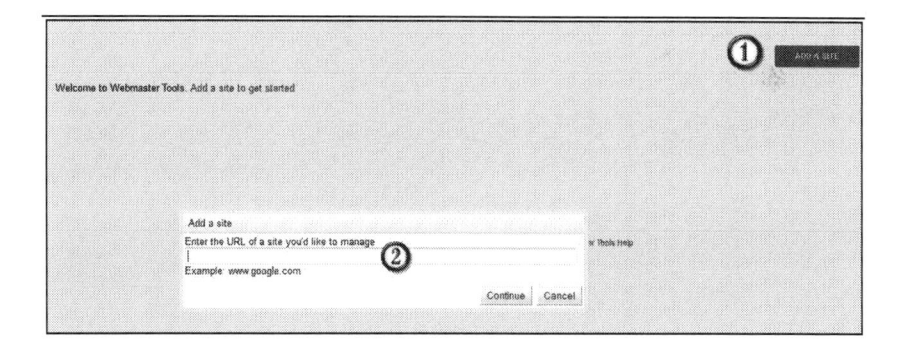

Next, you need to prove to Google that you are either the site owner or you are the site owner's agent. This step is necessary to prevent others from accessing information about your website without your permission. The simplest method to verify your site is to download a small HTML file they provide you with on this step, and then upload that file to your webserver. Once the HTML file is uploaded, click the Verify button.

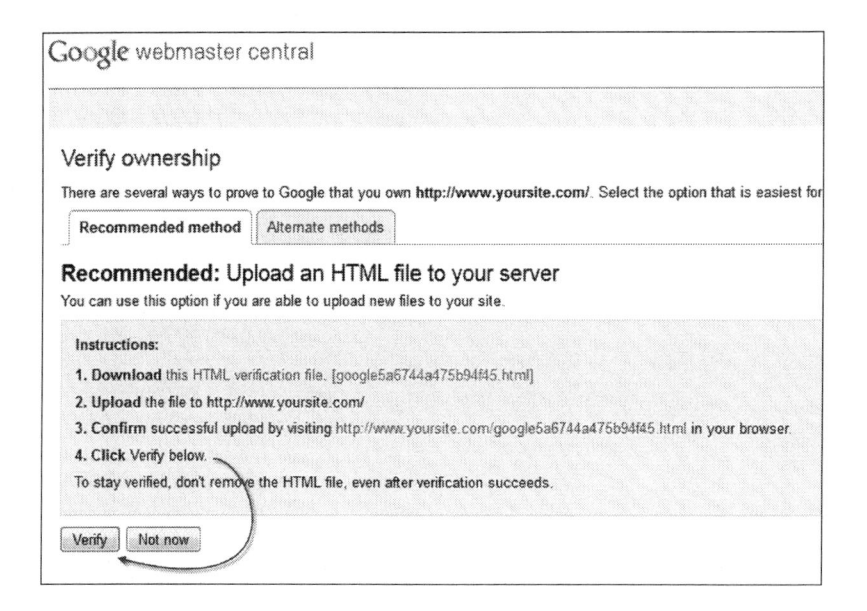

Preferred domain

You have arrived at the Dashboard! But before you start looking around at all this great new information, you want to specify your preferred domain.

Click on the link in the upper right of your window to go back to My Account. If this brings you to a general Google account page, click on Google Webmaster Tools. Now click the red ADD A SITE again. This time, add just **yoursite.com** (without the www). Again, you will need to verify your ownership, but since you already uploaded the file (or added the META tag) just click on the Verify button. You will be brought back to your Dashboard. Don't be alarmed to see that there is "No data available" for each of the tools. We are about to fix that.

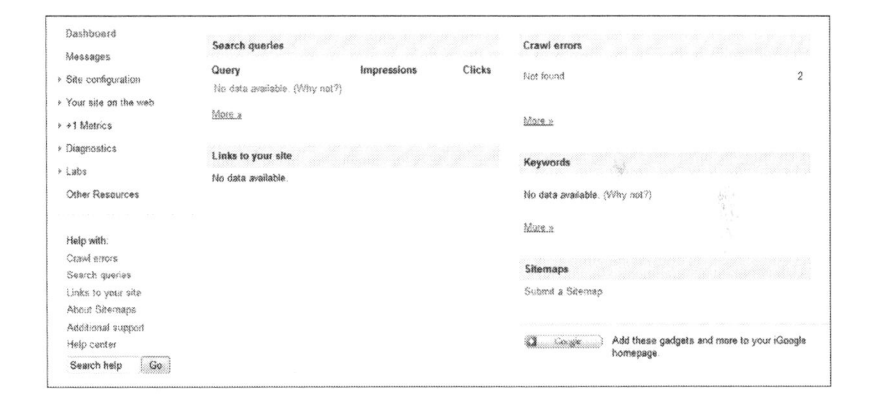

Now you have two websites in your account, one with the "www" and one without. You will need to choose which of the two you want to use as the "preferred domain." Google sees them as separate websites, and you do not want to dilute your SEO efforts. There is no right or wrong preference here – choose whichever way you like to see your site name.

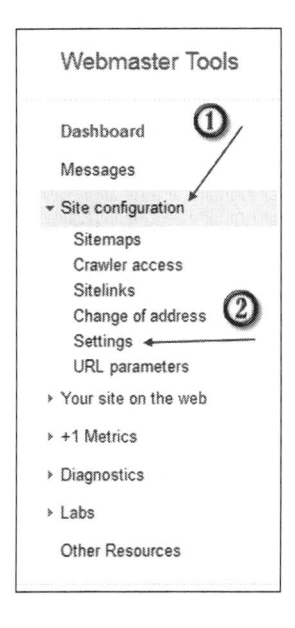

To specify your choice, go to Site Configuration, then Settings. Under Preferred domain, click the button next to your choice.

Remember to use your preferred name every time you reference your domain!

You also have the ability to choose a geographic target for your site. This is limited to the Country level. If you are a service-based local business, or perhaps a restaurant, you might want to target just your country. On the other hand, if you are selling a product globally, you'll want to leave this Unlisted.

Dashboard

Go back to your Dashboard. If your Preferred Domain is not listed here, click on the triangle next to your domain name in the upper right corner (1 below). Select your Preferred Domain from this list.

If you see errors here, click on the link that states the type of error. In this example, click on "Not found" (2) to see 2 URLs that are being linked to from external websites, but the pages are not on this site. If you find any errors, click on the name of the error and then click on the "Help with" links in the lower left corner to get some direction as to what to do. Any errors that you do fix will not be visible until after the next time Google visits (called "crawls") your site.

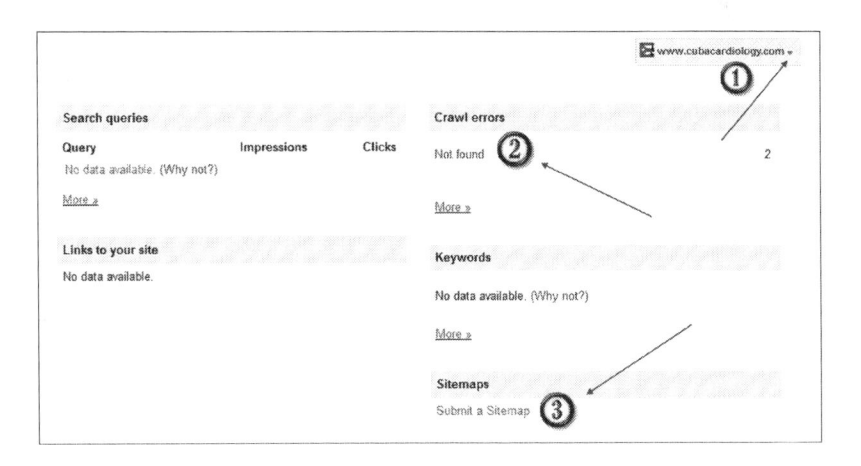

Submit your sitemap

It's very important to identify an XML sitemap (3 on previous page) for Google to use. This is not the same as a sitemap you might have on your website for your human visitors. The purpose of this kind of sitemap is to make it easy for the search engines to find all of your site's pages without having to crawl each of them. Ways that you might be able to generate an XML sitemap include:

- Dreamweaver,
- plugins on WordPress (search for "XML sitemap")
- http://www.xml-sitemaps.com/ (free for up to 500 pages).

WordPress sitemaps are created on your webserver. For all other methods, once you have built the sitemap, you'll need to upload it to the webserver. Then go to Site Configuration, Sitemaps. Click "Submit a Sitemap" and give Google its address: http://www.yoursite.com/sitemap.xml. (Note: enter this with your Preferred domain selection from the last step, with or without the "www".)

Google will immediately start processing your pages, and if you refresh your browser you'll see that it has counted the number of pages on your site (1 below). You should see a green check mark under the Status column (2).

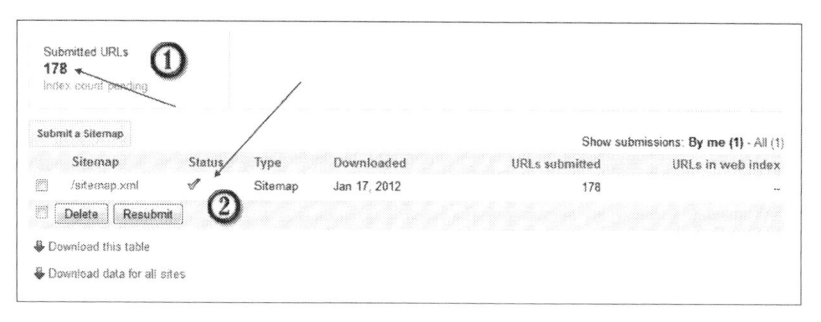

Be sure that the number of pages submitted agrees with the number of pages indexed. If these numbers are different, or if there is a red X under the status column, go down to the Diagnostics section to find – and fix – the problem.

Keywords and search queries

Go to "Your site on the web," then "Search Queries" to see the top queries (1 in diagram p. 45) that are sending visitors to your website. By default, this list is in order of how many impressions (2) you received: how many times your site was displayed in the results list when someone searched on the keyword. You can see the Average Position (3) of your site in the search, as well as how many times someone clicked on your listing and went to your site (4). In addition, you can see if your site is improving or declining for your keywords (% change).

Google does say that these results are "not exact" but they are the closest estimation we can get.

Your goal here is not only to have your website showing in higher Average Positions, but moreover, to maximize the number of times people are clicking through to your site. These are free clicks – you don't have to pay for them. Visitors decide whether to click on your listing, or someone else's listing, based on how your content is appearing in the results.

This is why your page title and META descriptions are so important. They need to include the keywords and compelling content that will entice visitors to click. If you are not getting the clicks, start changing the META descriptions.

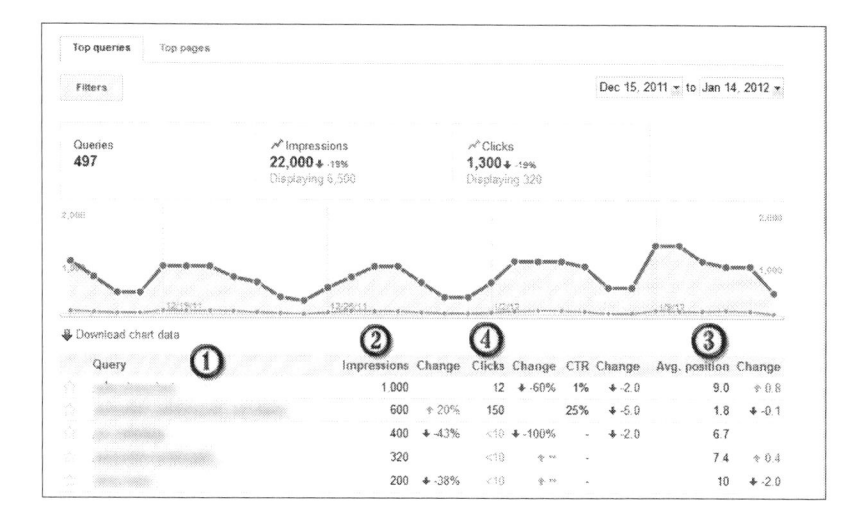

Links to your site

"Your site on the web," "Links to your site" will show you

- which sites are linking to yours,
- which page they are linking to,
- and what the link contains.

Getting links to your website is an important part of your marketing process because Google looks at these as votes for your site.

We also want to get links to **interior pages** of your site, not just to your **homepage**. First, you might have the information that your visitors are looking for in an internal page. Rather than take the chance of losing them because they can't find it, you want to link directly there.

Also, Google will put more credence in your site as an authority if others are linking to deeper pages. If this tool is showing that you have links to interior pages, that's excellent. If not, we'll be discussing some ways to improve this in Chapters 9 and 10.

Finally, **how** your data is linked is also important. This is called "anchor text" – what the text that someone is clicking on actually says. Ideally, anchor text should have keywords in it, not generic words like "Home" or "About Us." Again, we'll be discussing ways to improve this in Chapters 9 and 10.

Diagnostics

Google wants your title tags and META descriptions to be unique for each page. Go to "Diagnostics," "HTML suggestions" to see if there are any content issues with your website. Here is where you can see if you've properly created your Title tags and META descriptions. If Google finds anything that is missing, duplicated or problematic, this is where you'll see it. Of course, you'll want to fix these issues.

When Googlebot crawled your site, it found some issues with your content. These issues won't prevent your site from appearing in Google search results, but addressing them may help your site's user experience and performance.

Meta description	Pages
Duplicate meta descriptions	16
Long meta descriptions	0
Short meta descriptions	1

Title tag	Pages
Missing title tags	0
Duplicate title tags	13
Long title tags	0
Short title tags	0
Non-informative title tags	0

What if it says "No data available"?

If Google is not showing any data for your search queries, links, and other reports, it's possible that either your site is brand new, or Google didn't know enough about your site before because you didn't have a sitemap, links to the site, or both. Keep working on the concepts in this book and check back as you progress. You should see data within a few weeks.

CHAPTER 5: WORKSHEET

Google Webmaster Account

Website Name:
_____

Preferred URL:
_____ (with or without the "www")

Checklist:

☐   Created Webmaster account

☐   Verified URL

☐   Specified Preferred Domain

☐   Checked Crawl errors and fixed any problems

☐   Uploaded XML Sitemap

☐   Checked Search Queries and explored what pages are ranking well

☐   Checked Links to Your Site and explored where your links are coming from, and going to

☐   Checked Diagnostics/HTML suggestions and fixed any problems

☐   Set up a schedule to review the information here on a regular basis (monthly)

CAROL R HARKINS

6 Google Analytics

Knowing how your site is performing includes understanding

- how many visitors you are getting,
- where they come from,
- what keywords brought them there,
- where they are going on your site,
- how long they stay there,
- and numerous other measurements.

Google Analytics is a free resource that provides these answers within the bounds of some important limitations. There have been countless books written exclusively on Google Analytics and how to use and interpret them. This Chapter will provide you with some basics to get started.

Set up your Google Analytics account

Google has recently linked their Webmaster and Analytics accounts to make accessing this information simpler, but you will still need to create the Analytics account. To do so, go to http://www.google.com/analytics/ and click on Sign Up Now. Sign in with the same Google account (with user name yourname@gmail.com)that you did to create your Webmaster account.

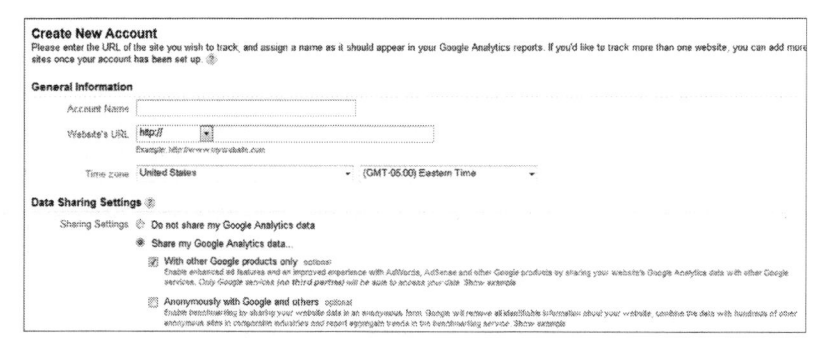

Click the Sign Up button on this new screen. Now you will assign an Account Name and then enter your website's address (URL). Remember to use the same one you created in your Webmaster Account, with or without the www. You will also specify your Time Zone.

Next you will be asked whether you want to share your Analytics data. This should be your personal choice.

While many find privacy concerns with sharing data with Google, you can use this data to your advantage by utilizing tools Google provides. You can deny any sharing, allow sharing only with other Google products, or allow anonymous sharing with Google and others for benchmarking purposes.

Finally, you will need to agree to their terms of service, then click Create Account.

Once you have completed these steps, you will be presented with your tracking code. First, you need to tell Google what kind of domain it is you are tracking. The majority of sites will be "single domain" which is the default.

Then you will copy and paste the code in the box – everything between and including the <script type="text/javascript"> to the </script> lines – just before the </head> line (in the head section) on each of your website pages (see diagram on next page). Be sure to include the code on all new pages that you create – otherwise Google will not be able to track them.

Once the code is added to your pages it will begin to collect information. Google generally takes 24 hours for this data to show up in their reporting section; however they currently have a Beta tool that provides Real-Time data.

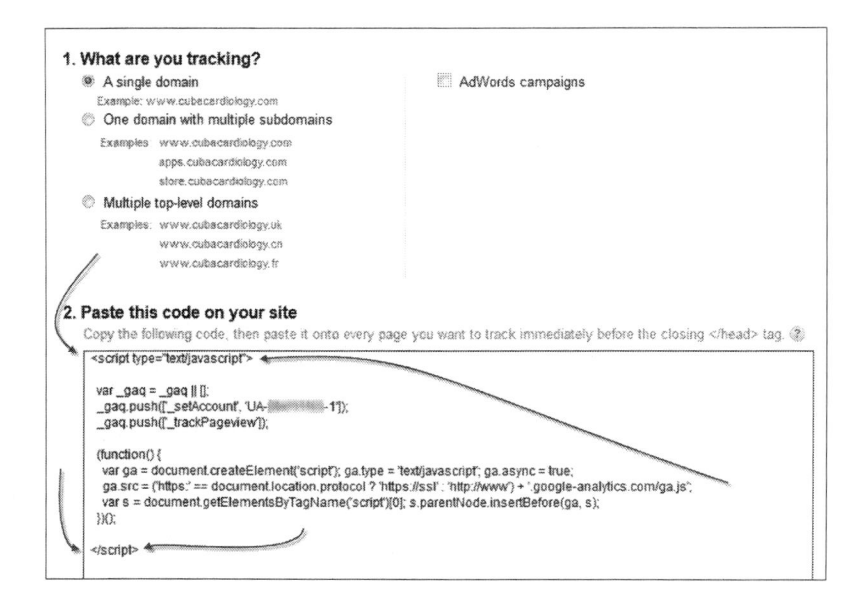

```
1. What are you tracking?
   ● A single domain
     Example: www.cubacardiology.com
   ○ One domain with multiple subdomains
     Examples  www.cubacardiology.com
               apps.cubacardiology.com
               store.cubacardiology.com
   ○ Multiple top-level domains
     Examples: www.cubacardiology.uk
               www.cubacardiology.cn
               www.cubacardiology.fr

   ☐ AdWords campaigns

2. Paste this code on your site
   Copy the following code, then paste it onto every page you want to track immediately before the closing </head> tag.
   <script type="text/javascript">

   var _gaq = _gaq || [];
   _gaq.push(['_setAccount', 'UA-*******-1']);
   _gaq.push(['_trackPageview']);

   (function() {
     var ga = document.createElement('script'); ga.type = 'text/javascript'; ga.async = true;
     ga.src = ('https:' == document.location.protocol ? 'https://ssl' : 'http://www') + '.google-analytics.com/ga.js';
     var s = document.getElementsByTagName('script')[0]; s.parentNode.insertBefore(ga, s);
   })();

   </script>
```

Accessing your analytics

Return to Google Analytics at http://www.google.com/analytics and log in. This will bring you to your Account Home, where you will be able to access all of your sites. Most likely right now there's only one site in the list. You'll see its tracking number and URL. Click on this entry and you'll see another link with the title of the site. Click again and you'll see the Visitors Overview section of the Standard Reporting tab.

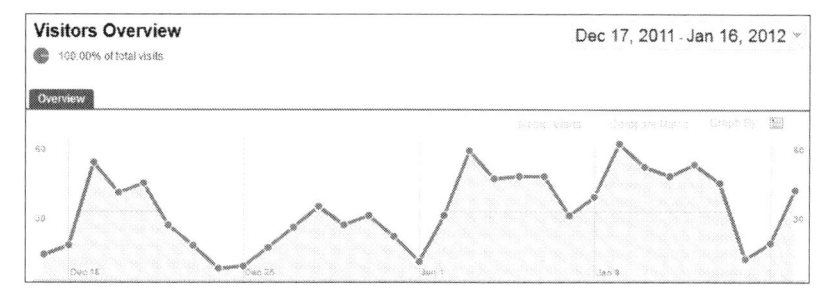

You can customize the date range of the visible data by clicking on the triangle to the right of the displayed range. A group of calendars will be shown, and you can modify the date range as desired.

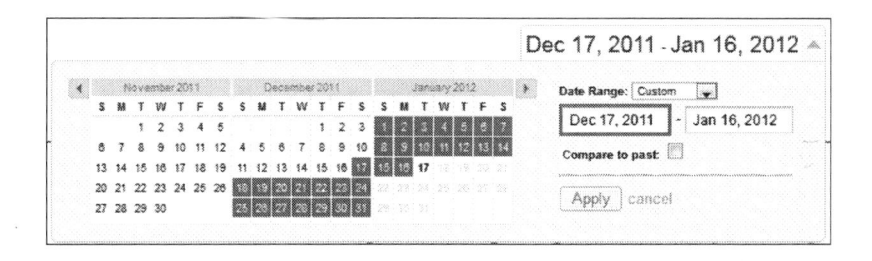

You can change the sort order of the listed data in all of these reports, by clicking on the column titles. For example, if you wanted to show the list from most to least, clicking on the column name will toggle this value.

Audience

This default overview is showing data about your Audience. This details information about people and visits, including:

- how many people visited your site,
- how many pages they viewed while they were there,
- how much time they spent on the site,
- and what the average "Bounce Rate" during that period was.

"Bounce Rate" is the percentage of your visitors who do not look past the page they came into your site on initially. Ideally you will want that metric to be less than 50%.

Above the list of these values is a graph which shows how that metric changed over the period of time you chose. Click on the small graph icons to the left of the metric name to display the graph for that metric.

Below these metrics are some general Demographics data. Click on the demographics type, such as Country, City or Browser, both for Desktop and Mobile, and the associated data will be displayed on the right. Click "View Full Report" and you can further "drill down" into the data (focus in on more detail).

You can also see data on how many of your visitors are repeaters, how many times they came back, and how long they stayed while there. The goal is for your visitors to keep coming back, since the more they see you, the better chance of doing business with you.

Count of Visits	Visits	Pageviews	Percentage of total Visits	Percentage of total Pageviews
1	757	2,419	80.02%	75.76%
2	95	413	10.04%	12.93%
3	37	99	3.91%	3.10%
4	22	150	2.33%	4.70%
5	16	51	1.69%	1.60%
6	6	28	0.63%	0.88%
7	4	7	0.42%	0.22%
8	3	7	0.32%	0.22%
9-14	6	19	0.63%	0.60%

Frequency & Recency — Dec 17, 2011 - Jan 16, 2012
Visits: 946
Pageviews: 3,193

Advertising

This section will be invaluable for tracking Google Adwords (PPC) campaigns. We discuss Paid Advertising in Chapter 13 of this book.

Traffic sources

This section shows where your traffic is coming from, and what keywords are actually bringing visitors to your site. "Referral traffic" comes from another website's link, or from a visitor who was on that site prior to coming to yours. "Direct traffic" can come to your site by typing your address into their browser's address bar, or by using a Bookmark or Favorite that they saved on their computer.

If you have your website set up to be your "Home" in your browser, then every time you start your browser and it displays your "Home" page, it will increase your Direct Traffic count. [**Note**: if you then go to another site, for example, Google, that visit will be added to your Bounces. You might want to re-think using your own site as your browser's Home since you could be increasing your Bounce rate by doing so.]

You can also see the keywords that resulted in your site being shown in a search, and where on average your site was listed. You can also see how many times someone clicked on your listing for that term, and on what pages they arrived once they clicked.

"Impressions" are the number of times your site was displayed as part of the result set.

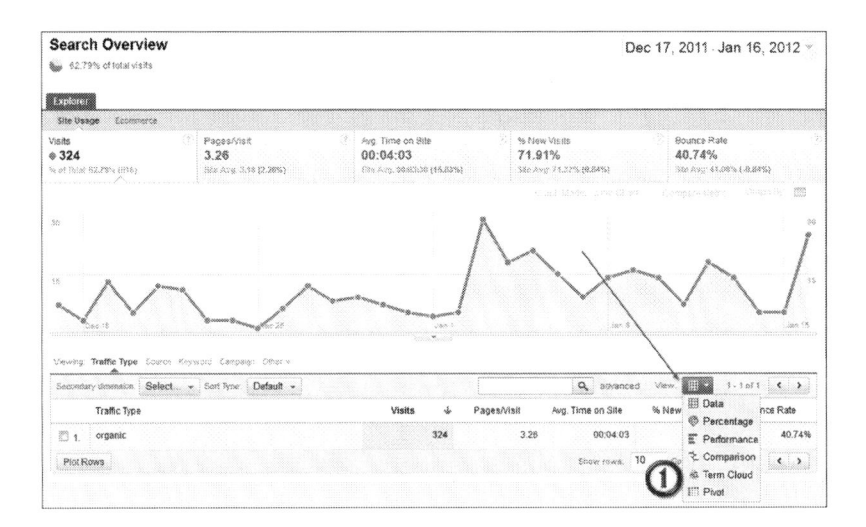

Use the Term cloud (1 in diagram above) to spot trends, based on whatever criteria you select. You can see at a glance what keywords are bringing visitors, which ones are causing bounces, and which ones are keeping visitors on your site.

Content

Here you can see what pages were viewed, and how often. If you aren't sure which page it is, click on the little arrow within the square icon to see the actual page. "Landing pages" are where people first come into your site; "exit pages" are where they leave. When the landing page is the exit page, that constitutes a Bounce.

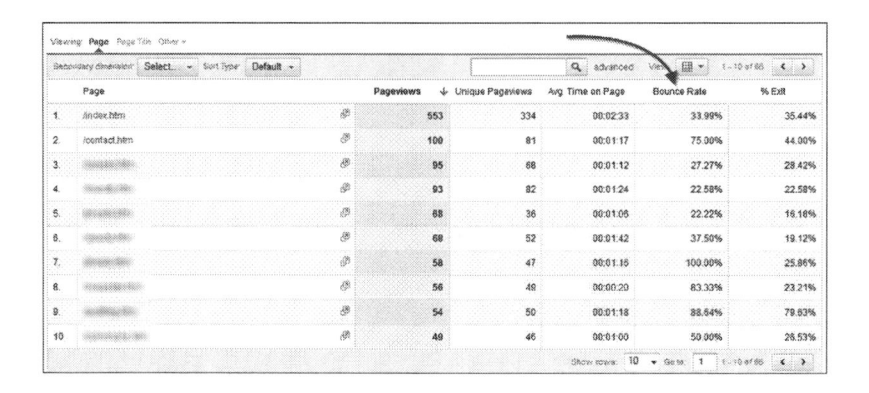

[table image showing Google Analytics page data with columns: Page, Pageviews, Unique Pageviews, Avg Time on Page, Bounce Rate, % Exit]

It's particularly useful to know landing and exit pages when they are not part of a bounce. Adding offers to reward visitors who have landed on a popular page can be very effective; adding forms to collect information from them on a page where many of them are leaving could be very informative. Another technique to use on exit pages is to add links to other related, relevant pages on your site. You may find they will continue on your site, rather than exiting, if you offer them more content.

You can also see measures of your sites' speed in this section, on a page-by-page basis. Google is using download speed as a criterion in their ranking, so if your site is taking a long time to load – or if a page in particular is slow – you will want to make changes to correct the situation.

You can customize the Dashboard with whatever reports you want to see when you first go to Analytics.

Conversions

This area allows you to define and track goals and is beyond the scope of this beginner's guide.

Using the Dashboard

If you click on the Home tab (see 1 in diagram next page) in Google Analytics, you will arrive at your Dashboard. You can use this area to customize the report segments that you find most beneficial. Add a report to the Dashboard from the Standard Reporting tab. You can create additional dashboards if you choose.

The dashboard widget can be further customized by the columns that you want displayed, and the type of graph or table that you want that data shown in. Click the little gear (2) in the **upper right corner of each widget** to see the customization interface.

If you don't want a particular widget in the dashboard, click on the gear, then Delete widget in the bottom right corner of the customization window. You can always add that widget back by going to the full report, or by clicking Add Widget at the top of the dashboard.

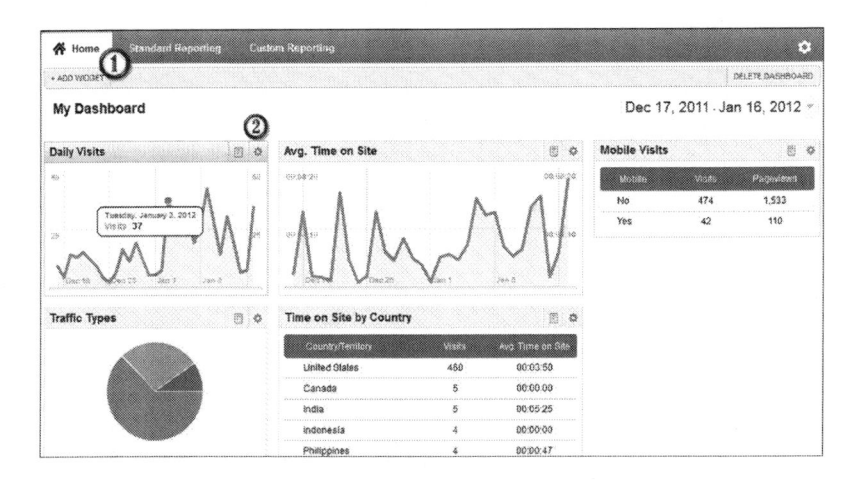

You can also jump directly to the full report for any of the dashboard widgets by clicking on the report icon, located to the left of the gear icon.

Drag the widgets around the page to rearrange them.

Associate Analytics with Webmaster Tools

If you see the following message, be sure you have a valid Webmaster Tools account for the domain. Then click on the "Set up Webmaster Tools data sharing" button. This will take you to a screen where you click "Apply" and then you should see a green "Success" message at the top of the screen. If you don't, follow the error message instructions. Be sure your domain names match (are you using "www" but you specified a preferred domain without?).

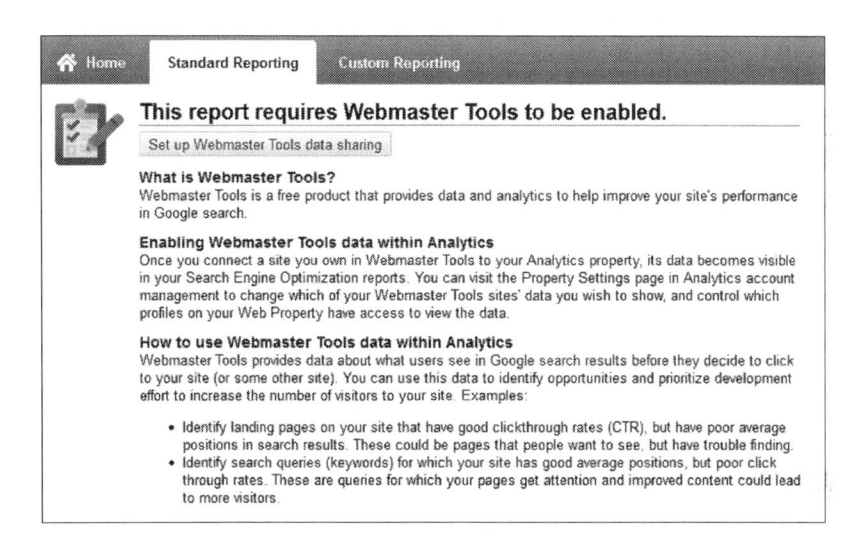

![Screenshot of Webmaster Tools setup screen showing "This report requires Webmaster Tools to be enabled" with information about What is Webmaster Tools, Enabling Webmaster Tools data within Analytics, and How to use Webmaster Tools data within Analytics.]

How Google Analytics works

Google Analytics works by activating a tracking code script on each page of your website. Each time someone requests one of your webpages, your webserver sends the file for the page to the visitor's browser or smartphone. The browser then displays the page by interpreting the lines of code on the page. When the script is run, information is sent to Google, including which page it is, where the visitor was before coming there (if that information is available), what kind of device (desktop/mobile/etc.) the page is being viewed on, etc.

Other analytics software works directly with the webserver logs. Webservers keep many of the same metrics that Google collects. The server logs can then be interpreted by applications to find out some of the same things Google Analytics does.

Unfortunately, these tools do not provide consistent data counts with each other. Usually webserver logs will show numbers that are much higher than what Google Analytics shows. This can be caused by
    1. Webmaster error: not including the script on every page of the website
    2. Visitors who don't have JavaScript enabled in their browser (and therefore Google Analytics will not run)
    3. Google Analytics does not count other search engine spiders and bots, but server logs do
    4. Differences in how each defines a "visit." A visitor can go to a website, look at some pages, and

then get distracted with something. Later – 10 minutes, 2 hours – the same visitor resumes the visit. Does that count as one visit or two? How much time must elapse in order for it to count as a separate visit? There is no universal agreement on this, and so different analytics tools will show very different values.

We recommend that you approach analytics from a relative perspective. Look at your own numbers compared to last week, last month, last year, using a consistent tool.

We suggest that you implement and follow Google Analytics now because it will provide you with many more ways of slicing and dicing your data than any other free server-based tool on the market. Plus, Google is continuing to add more features to Analytics that you will be able to use with the body of historic data that you will begin to collect.

There's much more to Google Analytics, but this should be enough to get you started!

CHAPTER 6: WORKSHEET

Google Analytics

http://www.google.com/analytics/

*Login name:*_____

*Password:*_____

Keep a record of some of your metrics. Add other metrics that interest you. Take action where indicated. Organic traffic is the number of visits you received from search engines. Do this on a regular basis!

Month				
# Visits				
# Pageviews				
Av. Time on Site				
Bounce Rate				
# Mobile Visits				
Organic Traffic				
Best Keyword				
Slowest Page				
Most Freq. Exit Page				

CAROL R HARKINS

7 Google Places and Local Search

What is Local Search?

With the continuing rapid increase in the number of webpages, it is no longer fruitful to search for a local service with a generic keyword set. Most people understand that typing **plumber** into a search engine will give them an enormous result set, most of whom are not in their local area. If you are in New Jersey, you probably want a plumber from New Jersey, not one from Tennessee.

Depending on what you are searching for, Google will make an educated guess as to where you are when you perform that search, and will deliver geographically specific results. You will need to change your location if you want to search another area. For example, if you are located in Massachusetts but your sister is in Maryland and you want to buy her a gift certificate at a restaurant, searching for **seafood restaurant** will show you those close to your location in Massachusetts. Change your location to your sister's zip code and your results will be local to her.

Since Google is showing results within the Web Search function based on location, it's crucial that your web presence completely and correctly define where you are located.

What is Google Places?

Google Places is a directory of businesses organized by their location. Every business that Google could find with a physical location is listed here, along with whatever basic information Google could find about the business.

> When Google Places first debuted there were many who thought that a small business didn't really need a website in order to have a web presence: they had a free page on Google Places. That has been proven to be short sighted. **Businesses with separate websites are now ranking higher in Google Places searches than businesses with only Places pages.**

Optimize your Places page

If you have not already "claimed" your Google Places page, do it now! You might find inaccurate information on your page, and you will find that the information is not "complete." Google's default page contains only a fraction of the information that they will allow you to add to the page, and they are continuing to make changes to their format, so what you see below might have changed.

In addition, if Google feels you are not following the rules, they will suspend your page. This is not something you want to take lightly. Yes, it's free to have a Places page, but the flip side of that is it can be frustrating to get any kind of customer service.

Establish your Places account

Use the worksheet at the end of this chapter to organize your information before you actually begin creating or editing your listing.

Then, go to **www.google.com/places/** There are two things you can do here, rate other places, and claim your own listing. You can (and should!) come back later to rate other businesses. Right now, click on the blue "Get started" button.

Log in with the same email address and password you have been using for your Webmaster and Analytics accounts. Then enter your main business telephone number, and click "Find business information." Be sure to use exactly the format they specify: (201) 234-5678. Do NOT use a toll-free number here or your listing will not be published.

> Google uses phone numbers paired with exact physical addresses to identify a business. Keep in mind they have many rules in place to prevent businesses from trying to scam their system. Many of these rules make it difficult for legitimate businesses to create their Places presence and they keep changing the rules frequently. Their Help system while improving can be extremely frustrating.

Google will then present you with a map, and any businesses in its database that match that phone number. In the event that your business is not shown on this step, you can choose to "Add a new listing." Otherwise, click the "Edit" button next to the one with the most relevant information about your business.

You will then see a screen where you can add and change information about your business. To prevent unauthorized changes to your business listing, Google has a strict verification process (which also changes from time to time). At this writing, you can choose either phone or postal mail verification. Phone verification is instant. Google will make an automated call to the phone number of your business, at which point you will be given a pin number to enter into your account. Postal verification can take several weeks, and requires your entering the pin number on the post card into your account.

Basic information

Your business name, address and phone number should already be showing here. Changing them will require additional verification.

Your business Name must be exactly as registered. Don't try to include a modifier or geographic term unless it's actually part of your name. For example, Joe's Tire Warehouse Inc. is fine, but if your business name is The Smith Corporation Inc., don't use The Smith Corporation Accountants or you will risk being suspended.

Be sure that your Name, Address and Phone Number are exactly the same everywhere you list them. That means "Rd" is not the same as "Road" and so on. Google sees variations as being different places, and you need the body of online information about your business to point to one and only one place. Additional information here includes:

- Email address
- Website address
- Description (200 characters max)
- Category

The most important part of your Places page is your Categories. These should describe what you are, not what you do. You can have up to five Categories. Use one of Google's defaults first, before you start creating your own. Be careful in using keywords as Categories. So for example, perhaps you are a cosmetic dentist and you provide your patients with Porcelain Veneers as well as Mini implants. You will want to use Cosmetic Dentist as a Category because it describes your business, and leave the veneers and the implants out of this list. Google will suspend your listing if you don't follow their guidelines.

Service Areas and Location Settings

You may not use a post office box as your address. Google wants you to use your actual, physical address which translates to GPS (Global Positioning System) values. If your business is home-based and you don't want to show the physical location on your

Places page – or if you are a service business that serves clients at their locations – you have the option to display a "Service Area" circle on the map instead of the red Google flag. In that case, choose "Yes, this business serves customers at their locations." Then you can:

- Specify a radius distance from a certain location
- List the areas you serve by name or zip code

Hours of operation

Be careful how you list these. Google is now using these hours as filters. If you give business hours as 9am – 5pm and someone searches for you at 6pm, Google may not show you as being "Open."

If instead you decide to show your business as being open 24 x 7, be prepared to answer calls at all times. Be aware that Google solicits comments from visitors, and if your business receives enough complaints that you are not open when you say you are, you risk having your listing suspended. Google does not like it when a business tries to "game" their system!

Payment options

Choose the ones that apply from their list.

Photos

Include relevant photos picturing your logo, location, products, and so on, but do not include anything that is either proprietary or belonging to another business. For example, if you are a Sporting Goods store, you should use your own logo, and you may include photos from inside your store showing your merchandise. But you cannot display the Nike logo, nor have a photo of only a Nike display inside your store.

Each image must be less than 1 MB in weight, and 1024 pixels by 1024 pixels in size. Use any of these formats:

- JPG
- GIF
- PNG
- TIFF
- BMP

Videos

It is very important to include a video here. First, upload the video to YouTube, then include the link to your video on your Places page. You can have up to five videos on your Places page.

Additional details

Here is where you can add information about your location (Parking available? Other languages spoken here?) Right now these are not being shown in your listing, but since Google is still giving you the option to include this information there is a likelihood that they will resume publishing it in the future.

Submit and verify

Click "Submit" and choose between phone and postal mail verification. Your listing will not appear in Google Places until you have completed their validation process.

Other directories

There are myriad other local directories where you will want to claim your listing and optimize your business.

At very least, be sure you are included in Yahoo! Local, Bing Local, Yelp, and Hot Frog. You can search Google for local directories in your particular industry, and make sure you are listed there too.

Be particularly careful that when you register for these directories, you use the exact Name, Address and Phone Number that you did with your Google Places page.

CHAPTER 7: WORKSHEET

Google Places

www.google.com/places/

Prepare your input in advance and save time building your page.

Company Name	
Address State Zip	
Main Phone	
Email Address	
Website	http://
Description (200 characters max)	
Categories (use Google's closest suggestion first)	1. 2. 3. 4. 5.
Service Area?	_____ mile radius from _____ OR Names, zip codes:
Hours of Operation	M T W Th F S S

Payment Options	Cash Check Financing	American Express Traveler's Check	Visa Discover MasterCard Google Checkout	Paypal Invoice Diner's Club
Photos	1. 2. 3. 4. 5.		6. 7. 8. 9. 10.	
Videos	1. 2. 3.		4. 5.	
Additional Details				

CAROL R HARKINS

8 Online Reviews

Why do I need online reviews?

One of the ways that the Web is now seen as a global community is in the Online Review arena. Since many services and products are available virtually, where the customer or consumer is not able to physically see them before buying, reviews can help them make decisions.

The power of reviews, compared to testimonials, is that they are published on third party websites and are therefore considered to be impartial. A business isn't going to put a negative testimonial on its website! But there is nothing to stop an unhappy customer from writing a negative review.

The potential danger in human nature dictates that someone is up to two times more likely to actually write a review when dissatisfied than when one is pleased with the product or service. No business is perfect, so negative reviews will happen.

That's why it's important to get positive reviews from your happy, satisfied customers.

Getting set up

First, you need to be sure that your business is listed on as many of the review sites as possible. You'll want to claim the listings where they already exist to be sure that the information is both accurate and complete. Google Places is becoming a very powerful review site, and they are also pulling reviews from some of the others. But you do not want to have **all** of your reviews on Google!

To get you started, we've included a list of some of the more prominent review sites in the Worksheet at the end of this Chapter.

Getting customers to write reviews

Most review sites require that the person writing a review have a (usually free) account. The reviewer will enter an email address and a user name, often his first name and last initial.

Most review sites have a policy against reviews being entered for a business by a third party. Be particularly careful with Google reviews. If you write (or enter) multiple reviews for your business and pretend that they are from other individuals, Google can readily detect this and they will suspend – or worse, ban - your account. Even if you have reviews written for you by actual customers, we don't recommend entering them yourself.

Some review sites, like Yelp, have policies against soliciting customer reviews. Their position is that a solicited review is going to be biased and they want only "natural" reviews on their site. As we've already established, however, human nature dictates that "natural" reviews are going to slant to the negative. So we encourage you to actively request that your customers write reviews for you. We don't suggest that you write them for your customers.

Reality ensures that for every ten requests you make, you should be happy with three actual reviews. One technique that works well is to offer a coupon or special discount to customers who write a review. The customer then prints the published review and gives it to you to receive your offer.

Set up a program where your staff or employees regularly ask happy customers if they would be willing to help your business by writing a review. You can provide a printed card with your offer, including the web addresses of the review sites where you want them to go. Just be sure that you have established your listing on the sites prior to launching your program!

Combatting negative reviews

What can you do if you see a negative review about your company? First, try to look at it objectively. Is there any grain of truth there? If so, can you approach the writer and offer to make it right? If you can honestly say that it is totally untrue, some of the review sites allow the business owner to write his side of the issue. If you can show that the reviewer is maligning your business without reason, you might be able to get the comment removed.

Remember that however you respond, your real audience here are the prospective customers that you don't have yet. Think about how you want to present yourself to your prospects and then act accordingly.

CHAPTER 8: WORKSHEET

Online Reviews

Here are some directories where your customers might be able to provide reviews for you. You'll want to create or claim your business with each one. Be sure to use the exact same address (citation) that you used with your Google Places account.

- ☐ AllPages - www.allpages.com
- ☐ B2B Yellow Pages - www.b2byellowpages.com
- ☐ BBB - www.bbb.org/
- ☐ Best of the Web - botw.org/
- ☐ Bing Local Listing Center - www.bing.com/local/
- ☐ BusinessFinder - businessfinder.com/
- ☐ Citysearch - www.citysearch.com
- ☐ CitySquares - citysquares.com/
- ☐ Craigslist - www.craigslist.org
- ☐ Hot Frog - www.hotfrog.com/
- ☐ InfoUSA - www.infousa.com/
- ☐ Insider Pages - www.insiderpages.com/
- ☐ Judy's Book - www.judysbook.com/
- ☐ Kudzu - www.kudzu.com/
- ☐ Localeze - localeze.com/
- ☐ MagicYellow - www.magicyellow.com/
- ☐ Manta - www.manta.com/
- ☐ MerchantCircle - www.merchantcircle.com/

- ☐ Superpages - www.superpages.com
- ☐ Yahoo! Local - local.yahoo.com/
- ☐ Yellow Book - www.yellowbook.com/
- ☐ Yellow Pages - www.yellowpages.com/
- ☐ Yelp - www.yelp.com/

9 Article Marketing

What is Article Marketing?

The idea behind Article Marketing has been used for years in print media. A business will write an article on a related topic of interest about its industry and have it published in an industry or general interest magazine or newspaper. The business is not paid for writing the article, but the intent is for the resulting publicity and status as an expert to cause increased business. For example, a hair dresser could create an article about the "Top Seven Secrets to Beautiful Winter Hair," or an elder attorney might write about "What You Don't Know About Your Assets Could Negatively Affect Your Future Long Term Care."

Internet Article Marketing

Article Marketing is an effective technique for getting links back to your website. It also promotes you, the business owner, as an expert in your field, and garners more traffic directly to your website from those who actually read your article.

Writing the article

What you write about will depend on your audience. Go back to the personas that you developed in Chapter 2. What is their unique pain? What do they want to know? What problems do they want to solve? Answering these questions will give you ideas for your article topics. You should be able to employ some of the keywords you are targeting from Chapter 3 as well.

The body of the article must of course deliver on the promise of your title. Be sure to use your keywords here as well, just as you would in on-page SEO. Your articles can be anywhere from 150 to 500 words, with a "sweet spot" at 300 words.

Spend some time crafting your article's title. It needs to engage your readers immediately – or else they are not likely to want to read the article itself. If possible, include your keywords in the title. Tell the readers what they are going to get out of reading your article – or what they will lose by not reading it (see the two examples above). If you can make the benefit of reading the article measurable, that's even better. For example, "How I Save Clients up to $300 Each Month on Their Mortgage" will attract more readers than "Refinancing Your Home" will.

Resource Box

This is the part of your article where you are able to link back to your website. You will in most cases not want to link to your homepage, but rather to a page within your site that relates to the article topic. Best, have an offer on your site for a free whitepaper or other report in exchange for the visitor's email address. Now you can increase your mailing list in addition to increasing traffic to your site.

Depending on the restrictions of the article directory where you are publishing your article, you can either use a plain text link back to your website, or an anchor text link. The difference in creating these links is:

Plain text link:
http://www.yourdomain.com/exactpage.htm

Anchor text link: <a href=http://www.yourdomain.com/exactpage.htm> Target Keyword</a>

We recommend that you use both of these kinds of links, if possible, in Resource Boxes that allow you to include two links.

Submit your article

You now need to have the article published in a quality article directory. There are many of these on the web, including Ezinearticles, Article Dashboard, Articles Base, Article City, Buzzle, and Hubpages. There are also hundreds of niche article directories which you can find by looking on Google.

Be sure to check the editorial guidelines before submitting your article to a directory. They will tell you how you need to write the Resource Box as well as other rules you'll want to follow.

It's not recommended that you submit the same article to multiple directories. Google will detect the "duplicate content" and you will get credit for only one backlink. Also, the article directories themselves want the content they are carrying to be unique. If you do decide to submit the same article to multiple places, don't forget to vary the content and links in your Resource Box.

Be sure to spread out your articles among several of the directories going forward. Rather than having 30 articles on Ezinearticles, ten each on three separate article directories will be more beneficial. Google wants variety as well as quantity.

Spinning articles

Article spinning involves creating different versions of your unique article by replacing words, sentences and paragraphs, resulting in new, unique articles. The purpose of this is to be able to publish the articles to multiple sites and receive backlink credit from all of them. Article spinning is beyond the scope of this book.

CHAPTER 9: WORKSHEET

Article Marketing

From your personas (Chapter 2)
What is their unique pain?
_____

What do they want to know?
_____

What problems do they want to solve?
_____

From your targeted keyword list (Chapter 3)
List some keywords that you will include:
_____

_____

Now brainstorm some article topics. Don't worry about getting the title exactly right at this point, just get down some ideas:
1.
2.
3.
4.
5.
6.
7.
8.

Create a sample Resource Box. You should have numerous Resource Boxes that you use for different articles. The Resource Box should be no longer than 15% of your article length.

Your name:

Website URL:

Your Unique Selling Proposition (1 – 3 sentences):

Your Call to Action (get a free ebook, mp3, whitepaper, etc.)
You can use an additional URL here.

10 Video Marketing

Most people like watching video – entertaining video, of course. It's been shown that videos can rank on Google for keywords such as those you are targeting. With the advent of the Flip video camera and other compact video cameras, there's no reason why you can't add Video Marketing to your marketing plan. In fact, Video Marketing is an extremely effective way to get links to your site, high volumes of traffic, and actually make sales.

While you can hire a professional video production company – and if you want a commercial to run on TV, you should – to get started with video marketing you just need a few basic, inexpensive pieces of equipment.

Equipment

First, you need a **camera**. A Flip HD or Kodak Touch camera, or an inexpensive webcam, will allow you to make simple videos for the web.

Add to that some sort of **tripod** or way to anchor the camera when you are filming. The exception to this would be if you're shooting an action scene. But mostly you will want to position the camera and shoot from that vantage. We recommend Gorillapods, which are small, inexpensive and reliable tripods that are as portable as the Flip camera.

You may be able to shoot without using special **lights**. Just remember that lighting is an integral ingredient in good photography. If this is the first time you are filming in a certain location, do a short test video to be sure that there's enough light for viewers to see your video.

Finally, you might want to consider an **external microphone**. While the Flip won't accept one of these, some of the other compact cameras, such as the Kodak pocket video cameras, will allow you to plug in a lavaliere mic. Be sure to turn the microphone on to test the volume prior to making your video.

Topics

Just as with Article Marketing, you need to create a video around a topic that is of interest to your target audience. In fact, you can use your articles as topics for your videos. However, you want to keep each video tightly focused, and between one and three minutes, tops.

Why not create a series of short videos on a topic? You can begin with a problem (what does your audience want?), and then briefly establish your credentials (why should they listen to you?). Next, give the solution – but not so much that they can do it without your help!

Maybe you do want to provide a step-by-step "how to" video, with detailed instructions on special techniques, because you sell the raw materials. Or you are selling a product and you want to create a "how to use it" video.

You could also create a video FAQ (Frequently Asked Questions) about your niche. Have a second person ask you the questions – on or off camera – and you as the expert provide the answers. This would also make a great "series" of videos.

Consider making a "slideshow video" of still images and words that tell your story.

Finally, **end with your call to action**, and include your website address. You can create a text box like the Resource Box in Article Marketing that displays your web address and phone number on the screen.

Just as with Article Marketing, be sure you are targeting keywords that are relevant to your business.

Tips on creating the video

- Whether you are in front of the camera, or just the voice over explaining how to do something, you need to keep your voice upbeat and energetic if you want your audience to watch until the end.
- Make the video entertaining!
- Be sure your background is clean and free of clutter. Consider purchasing a black drape or a Shoji screen if you are filming indoors.
- Do film at a time when there's no additional background noise, like construction work outside your window, or a barking dog or crying

baby. Yes, you're an amateur, but your video doesn't have to advertise that!

- Don't wait until the video is perfect. This is not the time to be a perfectionist, or you'll never finish it. Just get your video online before your competition does. Each video you publish will be better than the last one.

Publishing the video

YouTube is the largest video sharing site as of this date. Uploading your video to YouTube will make it visible to your friends as well as to the world. Be sure to name the video file with whatever keywords it is targeting.

You will need to establish an account at YouTube, and create a "channel" where you will want to publish all of your videos related to your business.

When you create the title and description of the video, use the same keywords. Just as with Article Marketing, craft the title so viewers are curious about what you might have to say on the topic. Include a link back to your website, and just as with the Article Marketing Resource Box, link to an internal (non-homepage) part of your website wherever possible.

Sharing the video

Once the video is on YouTube, share it with your friends from your YouTube account. Email its address to your list, and announce it on your Twitter and FaceBook accounts. The more views the video has, the higher YouTube will rank it – and the better chances you have of ranking highly for your targeted keywords on Google.

Also, embed the video on your own website. This gives you two benefits. First, it will increase the time visitors spend on your site, which is one of the metrics tracked by Google. Second, the number of times the video is viewed on your own site is added to the YouTube totals, which will help the video rank for Google. You can also incorporate your video into a blog post.

Beyond YouTube

While YouTube is the biggest video site, it's not the only one by far. Check out Blip.tv (if you are producing a series of videos), Dailymotion, Flickr, Metacafe and Viddler. Each of these requires that you have an account. Some of them offer paid accounts for additional features, but the free accounts should be sufficient.

CHAPTER 10: WORKSHEET

Video Marketing

Create a **YouTube Channel**: http://www.youtube.com/
Use your Google account to log in, even if you have never been to YouTube with these credentials before. YouTube is owned by Google, and will accept your login.
Channel name (letters and numbers only):
_____
Video **file name** (be sure it has keywords in the filename):
_____
Title (catchy, with keywords)
_____
Description (start with your website address, then your exact citation from Google Places. Then a text description with keywords)
http://_____
Citation:
_____
Text:
_____
_____

Tags (include keywords! Do not let YouTube choose your tags.)
_____

Category:
Autos & Vehicles
Comedy
Education
Entertainment
Film & Animation
Gaming
Howto & Style

Music
News & Politics
Nonprofits & Activism
People & Blogs
Pets & Animals
Science & Technology
Sports
Travel & Events

CAROL R HARKINS

11 Blogs and Why You Need One

Simply stated, a blog is the easiest and fastest way to get fresh content onto your website. Why is fresh content important? Because Google puts a gigantic weight on how relevant and fresh your site's content is. You can optimize your website perfectly, but if you never add new content, you might as well say goodbye to your investment.

Where should you host your blog?

The first requirement of your blog is to be sure it's hosted on the same domain as your website. Free blogs such as Blogger (even though it's owned by Google) and Wordpress.com are nice, easy, and the price is right. But free blogs are **not on your domain**. Even if you can add your name to theirs, like yourdomainname.blogspot.com - it's still **their** domain. So your domain will not benefit from all the fresh content and keywords, unless your blog is actually on your domain. Plus, you are limited as to the functionality you can use on these free platforms, so having your own blog is even more important if you want to take full advantage of what's available.

What platform should you use?

We strongly recommend that you create your blog on the WordPress platform (http://www.wordpress.org). It provides great SEO tools for your posts, as well as extensions, called plugins, you can use that will really pull your blog together. There is a huge community already using WordPress, so there is a strong support system available if you have questions or problems.

There are myriad themes available, many for free, that you can use with WordPress. But be sure that whatever you choose as a theme, your blog needs to have the same basic look-and-feel as your website. You want visitors to the blog to know where they are. Whether they come to your website first and then your blog, or vice versa, consistent branding is important.

What are categories?

Your blog should be organized into logical content sections, also called categories. They are like a table of contents for your blog. Use your general keywords for categories where possible. Ideally you will want to have seven to nine categories, although a few more or less is not going to be disastrous! For example, if you own a dog training business, your categories might include Dog Training, Dog Health, Myths, Tips, Equipment.

Just as you would if you were writing a book, strategize what your blog is going to be about. Before you start actually blogging, decide what your categories are going to be, and then define them within the blog.

Going forward, assign a category to each post that you write. If you don't remember to assign it, WordPress will automatically assign the post to the default category (often "Unassigned"!).

Eventually you will want to have dozens of posts per category. If you find that a category has only one or two posts, you might want to either write more on that category, or reclassify the posts into another existing category and then delete that category.

Visitors to your blog should have the ability to see all of your posts in any of your categories by clicking on the category name.

How about tags?

Tags are more like index words that are a form of "micro navigation aids." They are not used by search engines at this point, but you may want to include them for your visitors' benefit. If you create a "tag cloud" in the sidebar or footer of your blog, you can give your visitors an instant sense of exactly what you are covering here.

In the dog training example above, some tags might be puppy training, winter safety, dog bite prevention, dog collars, and so on. If of course you find that you could write dozens of posts about one of these, you might want to re-classify it as a category rather than a tag.

Tags are used to describe your post in more detail than categories. They should be very specific. There is no limit to the number of tags you can create for your blog. Unlike categories, the use of tags is optional.

Set up a plan

The worst thing you can do with a blog is to create one and then abandon it. Have a plan in place to determine when you are going to write, on a regular basis. Build it into your calendar. Try to blog at least twice each week. A blog entry doesn't have to be long and elaborate. It's also ok to include something "off topic" periodically. A blog is your company's voice. So including occasional posts that round out your mission is really important.

If you have several employees, you might want to designate one of them to do the blogging. If you're a sole proprietor, it's another job for you. Of course, you could hire someone to do your blogging, but I would caution you about doing that because no one is more passionate about your company and your field than you are. It will show!

Brainstorm topics

Where will you get ideas about what to write? That's always a big concern among first-time bloggers. Again, go back to your personas from Chapter 2. What interests them?

You can write about what's new in your field, at your company, some special aspect about a job you are doing. You can write an educational piece.

Get ideas about what's trending now in your field by doing a Twitter search, then put your own opinion about it on your blog.

You can also write posts to publish in the future. For example, you could set aside 30 minutes each Monday morning and write two posts. Publish one of them immediately, and schedule the other to be published on Thursday. If something of note happens during the week, you can always post a third time.

How long should my posts be?

Just as with Article Marketing, there is no magic number of words that you must have in every post. A short but interesting 75 word post is better than no post. An interesting 600 word post will also keep your audience's attention. If you want to keep your posts in the 250 word range, that's not a problem either.

Remember that a post does not have to be perfect, although running it through a spell checker – and proof reading your grammar – should never be skipped. Getting your personality out there, along with your keywords and most importantly, your content, is what blogging is all about.

CHAPTER 11: WORKSHEET

Blogs

Structure the Categories for your blog. Write down some topics for posts. Create a calendar for posting.

Blog Name:	
Categories	1.
	2.
	3.
	4.
	5.
	6.
	7.
	8.
	9.
Potential Topics Brainstorm with staff/ What's new in your field/	1.
	2.
	3.
	4.
	5.
	6.

Set up a calendar in advance for posting each month.
Sample Calendar
Month: _____

1	2 Post about Category 1	3	4 Post about trending news	5	6 Post about Category 2	7
8	9	10 Post about something new in your company —an offer, special, or new product, etc.	11	12 Post about Category 3	13	14
15	16 Post about trending news	17	18 Post about Category 4	19	20 Post about Category 5	21
22	23 Post about Category 6	24	25 Post about trending news	26	27 Post about something new in your company	28

29	30	31 Post about Category 7	**Notes:** **Topics for next month:**			

12 Mobile Marketing

Whether or not you own a smartphone, many of your prospective customers and clients do, and they are using their smartphones to find businesses such as yours. There are two major parts to Mobile Marketing: mobile websites and text messaging, or SMS.

Mobile Search

Google maintains a separate index for mobile web properties. This includes mobile websites and Google Places. Smartphones come bundled with other mobile-specific search functions.

So how big is mobile search? Google won't disclose their numbers, saying "Mobile search is growing fast." However, industry analysts at comScore and other organizations estimated in mid-2011 that there were anywhere from 300 to 690 million searches per day being performed on mobile devices.

Google also said in mid-2011, as a result of a study they conducted with Ipsos OTX, that 74% of smartphone shoppers make a purchase as a result of their search use on the phone, and 88% of those looking for location information on their phone take action within a day!

All experts agree these numbers are going to continue to rise. If your business is not included in these mobile directories, you are invisible.

This underscores the need to be listed in all geographic-based directories, both the general ones and the ones that are specific to your industry. When you submit your information to these directories, they calculate your GPS coordinates based on your physical address. Whether a prospective customer is searching for a pizza shop or a frame store, the smartphone knows his precise location through its GPS capability.

The default search results that are delivered will be relative to the location of the smartphone.

Mobile Websites

On the positive side, the mobile index is right now much smaller than the legacy index of all webpages. Having your business listed in the local directories is a start, but it's no longer sufficient. A dedicated mobile website, properly optimized for your keywords, will probably rank higher in the mobile index than in the legacy index, if only because there is much less competition.

Also, Google gives weight to domain age (although not stagnancy, so the same rules of adding fresh content will apply). So this means that getting your mobile website online sooner will also give you the age benefit, should you create a new keyword rich domain name for the site.

Your mobile website does not need to include all the pages and information of your desktop website. For most businesses, five to ten pages will be sufficient. In addition to your homepage, you will want a Contact Us page.

Think of your prospective visitors, and what information they might need or want while out and about. That's the information which is most important to include on your mobile site. Are you a brick-and-mortar business? A mobile phone is perfect for including a Google map that precisely identifies your location, as well as to create directions from their current location to yours.

Remember (with the exception of tablets like the iPad) mobile devices are phones. Be sure to include easy-to-find buttons that provide "Tap to Call" functionality on every page. After all, one of your primary goals is to have your prospects contact you. This is a very effective way to capture their interest while it's hot.

While you are creating your mobile website, be sure to optimize it for SEO. Use unique, keyword rich Titles and META Descriptions. Google has a separate index which it uses for search on a mobile device. This index favors sites that are mobile-optimized, and is much smaller than the original Google index. This means that if you are part of the mobile index your competition is much less, and the ability to get to the top is much easier. It won't remain this way, so getting in early is a great strategy.

Important: Be sure that your mobile site loads automatically when someone on a mobile device tries to access your website.

Desktop websites as seen on mobile devices

Just in case you are not yet convinced that you need a separate mobile website, take a look at your site on a mobile device. These include phones like Blackberry, Android and iPhone, as well as devices like iPads. If your website has a Flash "splash page," your visitors will never see it on an iPhone or iPad. What's a splash page? A splash page is usually created as a "doorway" to a website and often contains motion items such as words that fly in and out, as well as other animations. It's not a good idea from an SEO perspective to have a splash page, and since iPhones and iPads do not display Flash, this is a particularly bad idea!

If your website doesn't have a splash page, but instead is using Flash in your navigation scheme, visitors on an iPhone or iPad will be able to see the page, but won't be able to move past the homepage. Again, not a good idea, because the number of iPhone and iPad users continues to climb.

Even if you are not using Flash on your website, you might be surprised how your site looks on a mobile device. Check your analytics to see how many of your site visitors are there for the first time. Now imagine seeing your website with tiny print, and not knowing exactly where to find what you need. Those repeat visitors who have seen your site in desktop mode have some chance of knowing where they want to go, but using tiny navigation can also be challenging. While the visitor can zoom in on the text to make it readable, once he has zoomed in navigating around the page becomes challenging.

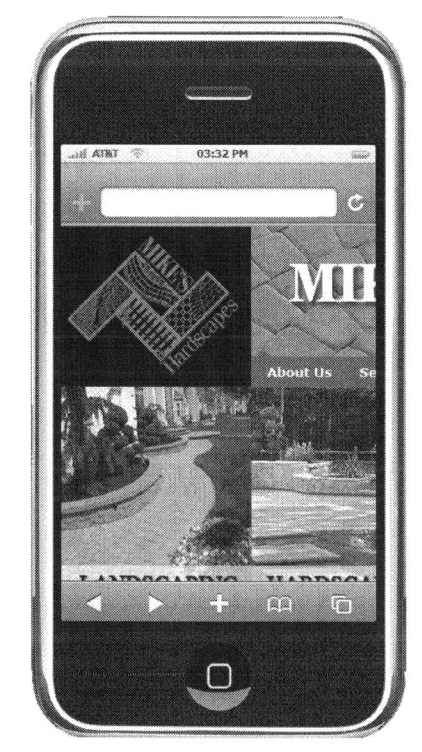

(Above left is a desktop website on a mobile device. Navigating around it isn't pretty.
Above right is the corresponding mobile website. The choice is clear!)

Text Messaging, or SMS Campaigns

Text messaging campaigns are very effective marketing tools. Mobile coupons have a redemption rate of 15% - 40%. Compare that to the 2% redemption rate of print coupons. There are a few reasons behind this. First, customers must opt-in or subscribe to your messages, so they are already expressing their interest in your services and company. Second, mobile messaging is real-time. As many as 95% of text messages get opened, and a large number of those are responded to within 5 minutes.

An SMS message is limited to 160 characters, although it can contain graphics such as coupons.

The ways to benefit from this are limited only by your imagination. As a restaurant, suppose you have over-ordered a particular special. You can send a coupon offering the first 10 customers who come in and order that special, and show the coupon on their phone, will get a special price/free appetizer/etc.

A hairdresser having a slow Saturday can offer discounted haircuts/manicures/etc. to anyone who comes in before 3pm.

Doctors and dentists can text appointment reminders, or reminders that patients need to call now because they are due for an appointment. An SMS program such as this can save staff a lot of time. Have to change the time of an appointment? Doctor running late? Patients will really appreciate a text letting them know they can spend the extra 30 minutes doing something useful to them, rather than sitting in the waiting room.

Pharmacies can send messages to customers when it's time to renew their prescriptions.

A store with overstocked items can offer a % off coupon. Having a slow night? A coupon to be used today could change that within the hour.

Many of these scenarios are strategies that can be used on a Facebook or Twitter account. The advantage to using SMS is that your customer base is more likely to open a text message on their phone, than to be on Facebook or Twitter, at any given point in time. The real-time nature of mobile marketing makes it ideal for building your customer base, increasing your profit, and decreasing your costs. And, if the recipients of your message don't have their phones on, the message will stay in the queue until they either read it or delete it. Since they chose to receive your messages, chances are it will be read.

Implementing SMS

In order to use SMS marketing, you'll need an account with a mobile marketing company. This company owns a "shortcode" like 12345, which is like a phone number. You'll choose an available KEYWORD that relates to your business. Then you'll need to create - or add - an offer to your website, billboard, or other advertisement. In order to receive the offer, your customers/prospects will need to text the KEYWORD to the shortcode on their phone (or enter your phone number into a website form). Your phone number will be captured in the database, the offer will be delivered, and a message will be sent back asking if the recipient wants to opt in for future offers and messages. Those who opt in will join your permanent list.

The mobile marketing company will charge you a monthly fee, plus a charge for a pre-determined number of outgoing messages that you then send to your list. Each message should contain information as to how your recipients can opt out if they no longer want to receive your texts.

CHAPTER 12: WORKSHEET

Mobile Websites

Look at your website using a smartphone such as an iPhone or Android. If you don't have access to one of those, use an online simulator such as http://www.testiphone.com/ or http://iphonetester.com/.

Now rate your mobile presence.

1. The site loaded quickly (only answer this if you are using an actual smartphone).

               YES   NO

2. A visitor can navigate the site (no Flash navigation elements or Flash splash screen).

               YES   NO

3. A visitor can **easily** navigate the site (major navigation elements large enough to both see and press).

               YES   NO

4. Visitors can **quickly** find content they need to know about your business if they are "out and about." Example: where you are located, how to call you, etc.

               YES   NO

5. Links are large enough to easily tap.

               YES   NO

6. The site takes advantage of telephone technology to make calling your business seamless (tap to call button)

               YES   NO

Score: 5 points for YES, 0 for NO.

25 – 30: You're ready for mobile!

15-20: You're limping along but that's not really good enough!

0 – 10: Red light! Get a mobile site NOW!

13 Paid Advertising (PPC)

What is Pay Per Click?

Pay Per Click (PPC) is the most frequently used vehicle of paid advertising. You have probably noticed the results displayed in a shaded area at the top, as well as to the right, of the regular or "organic" search results when you perform a search. These are paid advertisements. Most of a search engine's revenue comes from these ads. The advertiser pays for the ads based on how many times a visitor clicks on them, hence the term "pay per click."

While Google is the biggest fish in the PPC pond, Yahoo! and Bing also offer this type of advertising. Most keywords will cost less on the non-Google sites, but you will get correspondingly less traffic there too. Some business niches might do well to investigate using these but since we feel that the more traffic, the more customers and clients, we will talk about Google here.

Pay Per Click involves bidding on the keywords you want to be listed for. Bids can be as little as $.05, up to the neighborhood of $50.00. Some of the most competitive areas include the insurance industry, the loan industry, mortgage and attorneys, according to WordStream's 2011 study. You should recall the CPC (cost per click) values during your keyword research in Chapter 3, where the Google Keyword Tool showed you prospective click costs for position 1 for your keywords.

The more you bid, and the better your click-through rate is (how many people click on your ad relative to how many times it is displayed) the better your position is in the list.

Let us state up front that **PPC is not a beginner's tool** although anyone can create a campaign to drive traffic to his website. As a wise man once said, "A fool and his money are soon parted." PPC will absolutely drive traffic to your site, but whether it will bring you the right traffic – traffic that will convert to sales, customers and clients – is a more difficult task. Be careful or you can throw away a lot of money on traffic that doesn't raise your bottom line.

We include this chapter so that you can get a basic understanding of the technique and therefore be an educated consumer if and when you decide to use it – or to hire an expert to do it for you.

PPC basics

To start, go to the Google Keyword Tool online. This is actually called Google AdWords. After you sign in to your Google account using your now-familiar login credentials, you will put together a "basket" of keywords that are tightly related to each other. A notable difference from our keyword research in Chapter 3 is that this time we want to use Broad Match search with the Keyword Research Tool.

Then you will create your advertisement. There are volumes written about how to write an effective ad. These ads are tiny: 25 characters in the headline and

35 characters in each of two descriptive lines. The text in the ad must be relevant to the keyword group you are using it with. Google also has additional rules regarding the types of words you can and can't use, and all of this information will be available in help screens while you are creating the ad online. You can even choose whether your ad is going to be a plain text ad, an image ad, or a mobile ad.

Google's Keyword Tool will also show you traffic estimates based on the keyword you choose, the maximum you want to pay per click, and your daily budget. All of these are variables in the equation of what position your ad will be shown, how often your ad is shown, and even **if** your ad is shown. If your budget is low your ad might not be displayed on every search, and if your budget has been exhausted your ad will no longer be displayed at all.

Another factor that determines where your ad is displayed is its quality, measured by how many clicks you have received (how popular it is). The more popular, the more it will be displayed, the higher it goes – but don't forget that you are paying for each click. Ka ching!

Once your campaign goes live you will want to follow it closely with the various analytic tools that are located within your Adwords account.

PPC Strategy

- Always have at least two ads running at the same time. You want to see which one performs better. When you have a clear winner, give up the loser and write a new ad. Rinse and repeat.

- Aim for the 3rd or 4th position. Your costs will be much less than the top position, and you will get more real buyers than "tire kickers."

- Use geographic limitations so that your ads are not shown in places where you don't do business.

Other paid advertising

Banner ads are another form of paid advertising. These can appear across the top or down the side of websites. Before buying this type of advertising, determine how many impressions (how many times the page is viewed) they will guarantee you.

The main problem with banner ads from our perspective is something called "banner blindness." It has been shown in eye-tracking studies that people often don't actually see banner ads. They know they are ads and they literally don't see them.

If your website gets a lot of traffic you might want to make some additional revenue by offering banner ads to others. Just as you would want to know how many impressions you would be getting if you were buying a banner ad, your prospective buyer wants to know how many impressions you are going to offer them. That will usually dictate how much they are willing to pay you. The downside of offering banner ads is that you risk people leaving your own website before they have responded to your call to action.

CHAPTER 13: WORKSHEET

Pay Per Click

Before you begin a Pay Per Click campaign, do some basic calculations to get an idea of what you might see as a return on your investment.

Expectation:

_____ sales at $ _____ per sale = $_____
(should exceed your budget!)

Budget: (e.g. $1000.00) $_____

Time period: (e.g. 4 weeks)   _____

Hours for ad to run per day (e.g., M-F 7am – 11pm):
_____

Daily budget = Total budget _____ divided by

number of days _____ = $_____

Log in to the Google Keyword Tool, Traffic Estimator tab to complete the following:

Keyword: _____

Maximum cost per click you are willing to pay: _____

Average estimated Cost Per Click (CPC): _____

Total estimated daily clicks: _____ multiplied by

 number of days _____

= Grand total clicks: _____

[**Note**: Your actual click-through rate will depend in part on the quality of your advertisements. Your actual conversions will depend largely on the quality of your landing page.]

Actual conversions (number of sales) =
Grand total clicks (from above) _____ multiplied by your average closing rate _____ = _____

Actual conversions _____ multiplied by
Your average sale _____
= **Gross outcome of campaign** _____

Is this number likely to exceed your budget spent?

14 Summary

We hope this book has given you the framework on which to build your Internet presence, and that you understand this is not something that you will be able to accomplish and just check off on your to-do list. You will need to actively participate in the Internet marketing of your website in an on-going basis. When you do, you will surely reap the rewards.

The worksheets from this book are available online in PDF format. Download them at http://www.CyberGnarus.com/Internet-Marketing-Worksheets/.

We would also love to hear your stories about your challenges and your successes. Please email us at feedback@CyberGnarus.com. We may not be able to personally respond to every email, but we will be answering questions and highlighting successes on our blog, at http://www.CyberGnarus.com/blog/.

So now – go forth and prosper! Use what you have learned here to add value to your website for your own customers and prospects. Make your site more visible and attract more traffic. Create a community of followers by giving them something to benefit **them**, and when they need what you are selling, they will remember **you**. We are really only recreating the principles of our forefathers, but in a digital – virtual – framework.

Made in the USA
Charleston, SC
21 February 2012